Advance Praise

"I had to allow myself a lot of time to read it, even though time doesn't exist—but humor exists, even if there is no time to laugh."
—GROUCHO MARX

"I hope time exists, having read it- and had to laugh all the way through."
—JOHN LENNON

"All I can say is that I had enough time to read it, and to laugh for a long time."
—GEORGE HARRISON

"Time doesn't exist? I didn't know that. Give me some time to think about it."
—BOB HOPE

"I enjoyed it, and took my time to read it- but had a hard time in the beginning, because hard time is too hard to sit on."
—LESLIE NIELSEN

" I have it as my favorite book in my life after death."
—GENE HACKMAN

"I have it as my only book in my life after death, because the others I didn't have time for."
—GEORGE BURNS

"I love it, and will have it with me for eternity."
—FREDDIE MERCURY

"I... I had it in my hand with my watch that must have been stolen. Hear... hear me out on this—I had both the book and the watch together, and did not watch them. I could have, if I wasn't in the book."

—BOB NEWHART

"I couldn't have enjoyed it more, if I had more time, or not."

—JOHN CANDY

"I can tell you how much I liked this book. It is all I ever need to read, and all I ever need to know. How do I know that, I hear you asking? I am in the Mind of God as an aspect of life, having nothing but a life-healing experience—*as everyone else is*—although mine is completed. That is how I know, and I can give you one piece of advice—you can heal in life, or you can heal in death. It's not *either-or*, it's *either-and*, meaning it's going to happen, if you like it or not. My advice is to like it, because that is the way to heal it."

—GEORGE CARLIN

OTHER WORKS BY THIS AUTHOR

The Moment of Death

The 5th Secret

The 4 Secrets of the Universe

All About the Soul's Journey

The Book of Manifesting

Mysteries, Prophecies, and the Hollow Earth

The Lightness of Being

Sojourn

Poet Gone Wild

Poems of Life, Love, and the Meaning of Meaning

Infinite Healing

Poems and Messages for the Loss of a Loved One

Poems and Messages for the Loss of Your Animal Companion

You Bet Your Life After Death

Paul Gorman

Copyright © 2025 Paul J. Gorman
All Rights Reserved

 Year of the Book
135 Glen Avenue
Glen Rock, PA 17327

ISBN 13: 978-1-64649-512-2 (print)
ISBN 13: 978-1-64649-513-9 (ebook)

Cover images licensed from Alamy.
top (l-r): Leslie Nielsen, John Candy, John Lennon, Gene Hackman
center (l-r): Freddie Mercury, George Fenneman and Groucho Marx, George Harrison
bottom (l-r): George Carlin, George Burns and Gracie Allen, Bob Hope, Bob Newhart

No part of this publication may be reproduced, distributed, or transmitted in any form or by any means, including photocopying, recording, or other electronic or mechanical methods, without the prior written permission of the author, except in the case of brief quotations embodied in critical reviews and certain other noncommercial uses permitted by copyright law.

Disclaimer:
The author is not responsible for any absurdities, ridiculousness, or nonsense contained in this book. All comments resembling them are purely intentional. Any insights or laughter are for healing purposes only.

Contents

Foreword 1
Introduction 3

ROUND 1 7
"Would you have liked to live longer?
Why, or why not?"

ROUND 2 17
"What was your favorite breakfast?"

ROUND 3 35
"How could all you had done heal so many people,
and not yourself?"

ROUND 4 55
"What do I miss in life, that I cannot manifest
in heaven?"

ROUND 5 75
"How can I heal myself in my afterlife?"

Afterword 98
About the Author 99

Foreword

You Bet Your Life was a humorous "quiz show" that aired on radio starting in 1947, and then on television from 1950 to 1961. In the beginning, there were likely more people in the live audience than households owning a television.

The show was hosted by Groucho Marx of 'The Marx Brothers' fame, with his announcer George Fenneman. I first saw it as a rerun on television in the 1970s.

Even then, there were only 3 television channels, and the program was run late at night. All of the stations signed off at about 1:30 AM with a poem, while showing a fighter jet flying higher above the atmosphere. That alone would have cured any insomniacs still watching... until the annoying tone that came on to fill the programming airwaves for the next 5 hours.

That was if you lived close to a major city. Now you can watch *You Bet Your Life* episodes on your phone, at any time—and they are as funny as ever.

This book is a continuation of that program, with my channeled messages from Groucho and his mostly more contemporary guests who are also physically deceased—John Lennon, George Harrison, Bob Hope, Leslie Nielsen, Gene Hackman, George Burns, Freddie Mercury, Bob Newhart, John Candy, and George Carlin.

The chapters are similar to the television program, where Groucho asks each of the contestants a question, with a chance to win a prize if they say "the secret word." The dialogue and answers are always funny, and even hilarious—while often providing insights into life after death.

You will hear each one's voice and unique personality and sense of humor coming through in all of these quiz show rounds.

Announcer: "It's time for *You Bet Your Life After Death* with your host, Mr. Groucho Marx!"

Introduction

If you are familiar with the entertainment personalities on the cover of this book, you will hear each one's unique voice and sense of humor coming through in the following chapters.

This text will not likely lend itself to being an audiobook, though an A.I. version could very well recreate their actual voices. That would still require some work, because as Bob Newhart said in *The 5th Secret*, the timing in comedy has to be perfect.

I wrote, or channeled, the conversations in this book in early 2025 after completing *The 5th Secret: In the Universe that I Am*, which also includes dialogues with each of these personalities about their experiences in spirit world. The first chapter in this book is carried over from *The 5th Secret*, and that conversation is what inspired this book—and the title, which came from one of Groucho's first comments in that chapter.

It is clear to me that people do not die—just heal. We heal in life, or not—but our minds heal most significantly in death by losing our ego attachments, and earthly concerns. Spirits say that their healed Light Minds and bodies are as alive as ever. Laughter is healing, and I was lucky to have grown up knowing some of the work of these great entertainers.

Imagine having Groucho Marx, John Lennon, George Harrison, Bob Hope, Leslie Nielsen, Gene Hackman,

George Burns, Freddie Mercury, Bob Newhart, John Candy, and George Carlin—all together for a comical "quiz show."

Now they are all here together, and you can bet that their healed minds will have you laughing at life, and at life after death.

The first chapter, Round 1, is my dialogue with all of the guests, and Rounds 2 through 5 are in the format of Groucho's TV show.

It would be well for the individual to cultivate humor and wit, the ability to see even the ridiculous."

—*Edgar Cayce*

Round 1

"Would you have liked
to live longer?
Why, or why not?"

I'd like to ask all of our celebrity guests one question:

"Would you have liked to live longer?
Why, or why not?"

Mr. Groucho Marx, you can be the host. *You Bet Your Life* was your TV show in the 1950s.
All I can bet now is 'your life after death'. Let's ask both John Lennon and George Harrison. That was my TV format.
John and George, how are you both doing after breaking up? I could have bought your records, if I was still alive then.

Thank you, Groucho. I'll ask the questions now.
I still have more to ask John and George. How come I wasn't invited to be in your group?
I can sing, and I can dance—but not as well as I can sing because of a cigar that is stuck in my hand.
Maybe I can hold it over my head, and no one will see it.

Okay Groucho, I am going to be the host now of *You Bet Your Life After Death*.
I was just getting into the swing of things.
"I can dance, and I can swing—
   I'm in the Beatles, and I can sing!"

Thank you, Groucho. We'll come back to you later in the program.
The question to all of our contestants is:

"Would you liked to have lived longer? Why, or why not?"

John Lennon: I am a lot deader than I have been led to believe. I cannot be like George, and live forever.

What do you mean?
George has become a living legend, and I have become a dead one.

No, John. George has died also.
Died? I'll call on him so we can get together.

Were you unaware of his death?
I was. How did he die?

I will let you connect with him. Do you wish you could have lived longer? Why, or why not?
I had been alive for a long time, making me not need life as much as a child would, you know—but I could have lived on to see how my last album was received, not influenced by my tragic death.

That is a good answer. Your *Double Fantasy* album was released right around the time of your death.
I am asking the same question to George Harrison: "Would you have liked to live longer? Why, or why not?"
I can answer that one very easily. I would like it if I could have healed in my life, but I did not—so I prefer that I died, lowering my life expectancy, but I had not expected it to last forever anyway.

Thank you, George. The same question to Bob Hope.
All I can hope for was to not die again, because it wasn't pretty.

Would you have liked to live longer?
If I could avoid my own death, I would.

That answer is incorrect! Sorry Bob, you cannot avoid your own death. The same question to Leslie Nielsen: "Would you have liked to live longer? Why, or why not?"
I would like to live, but not longer. I was 6'1" tall.

Ha, ha, great answer. Now Gene Hackman. You have only recently passed away, but would you have liked to live longer?
I had lived longer than 99% of people, so having a longer life is not as important as having more love in my life—meaning, I would not necessarily have liked for it to be longer.

Another excellent answer. George Burns and Gracie Allen, same question: "Would you have liked to live longer? Why, or why not?"
George here. I lived longer than him, so I have to say that I lived longer than 99-point-9 percent of people, making my longevity make me a widower. Gracie died at a young age, and I missed her in my life, 99-point-9 percent of the time.

Thank you very much, George. Mr. Freddie Mercury, "Would you have liked to live longer? Why, or why not?"
I always have my music to live on in the hearts and minds of people, where I can feel their love of my singing and performing.

I am here, and I am there—so I am withholding my answer until I have heard all the others answer.

Alright. Let's move on. Freddie is in between and undecided. Mr. David Bowie, "Would you have liked to live longer? Why, or why not?"
I am always open to creating something new, so I am better off here in the spirit world.

Thank you, David. Next is Bob Newhart. Bob, "Would you have liked to live longer? Why, or why not?"
I could have lived longer in my corpse-like state, but it would have frightened a lot of people. Hear... hear me out on this. I could have frightened a lot of people on Halloween, and they would not have wanted to take my candy.

Ha, ha... speaking of candy, Mr. John Candy, "Would you have liked to live longer? Why, or why not?"
I lived pretty large, if you know what I mean. Could I live large, and also live longer? I don't think so.

I mean, I could, but it would not be that easy to do. It is possible, but life has to be completed in a certain period of time.

Thank you, John. Freddie, do you have an answer yet?
I do, darling. How could I not give you the answer you want? I would like my life to go on, and on, and on— in all of its fabulous highs, and desperate lows— making a line that is never flat, like all of my songs.

Great answer. Thank you, Freddie. Now for our final contestant, Mr. George Carlin. George, "Would you have liked to live longer? Why, or why not?"

If I lived longer, I could have all of my healing done in one day by loving myself, in all of my insecurity.

How could I be insecure if I could go onstage, with nothing to support me but an audience?

An audience is only a reflection of what you have presented to them. It is ALWAYS, ALWAYS, ALWAYS the same. You are only going to get back what you put out.

How can I get the audience to love me? By putting out love into the audience. It is a simple input, which gives you an output—making it always healing if you put what you want into it. What do I want? I'll tell you what I want. I am God, and I don't want anything.

I want you to heal, and for you to not want anything also. That makes me WANT something. So, if YOU heal, I will not want ANYTHING.

I can heal myself, and in my healed state, I am not wanting. I am God, illuminating in you having been healed.

I am healed, and you are healing. If I am healed, and you are healing—it means we cannot be one—in MY mind, or in YOUR mind.

How can you be one in God Mind? Want nothing and be ONE thing—LOVE.

Now we are one. I am in your thoughts, and in your prayers.

Excellent answer. Thank you, George. Now back to Groucho Marx: "Would you like to have lived longer? Why, or why not?"
I've certainly had enough of death, I'll tell you that much.... not that I'm complaining, being God and all.

I can have and be whatever I want, but I don't want anything. Now it gets interesting, because how can I become anything if I don't want to?

That's how come I have you in the world. You want everything, but don't know what you really want.

How can I let myself have nothing, you are asking? Because everything you want IS nothing—except for God's love, which is everything.

How can I get some of God's love? I thought you'd never ask. It is inside of you, and all around you.

It is coming out of your heart into the world in having loving thoughts about it- which includes having yourself in it as its receiver, and its projector. How's THAT for a conundrum—unless you are God and don't have a need for it—because you ARE it?

Am I making it clear now? Let me ask your question another way. How can I be all loving while I am living, even if my life is ending?

It is all I can be, even if you cannot want for anything more. It can be, because I am asking you to be ONE with me.

Thank you to Groucho, and to all of our guests on *You Bet Your Life After Death.*

Round 2

"What was your
favorite breakfast?"

Announcer:	Welcome back to our contestants on *You Bet Your Life After Death*. Tonight's question is, *"What was your favorite breakfast?"*
	For tonight's contest, there is a secret word [**JUICE**] and our spirit guests are asked not to see it on the screen.
	Contestants who say the secret word will win the top prize of $1,000.
	We will begin with Mr. Bob Hope, who lost that last round of questions.
	Here is your host, Mr. Groucho Marx.
Groucho Marx:	How can a contestant have a need for $1,000? I'd like to know because I want to win $1,000 too.
	How about you, Mr. Hope? Can I call you Bob?
Bob Hope:	Yes, you can call me anything having "Bob Hope" in it. I have $1,000, that's why they call it "a grand."
Groucho Marx:	I could be "a grand," like a grandfather, but I wouldn't have $1,000. I'd have grand larceny if it was stolen.
Announcer:	Tonight's question to Bob Hope is, *"What was your favorite breakfast?"*
Bob Hope:	I liked eggs, and having them cooked in an omelet having all kinds of other

	things in it, like mushrooms and peppers.
Groucho Marx:	"All kinds of other things in it?" Do you mean like car tires and things like that?
Bob Hope:	No, I mean like onions, and having some toast with it.
Groucho Marx:	Is that all? Don't you get thirsty having to take the tires out of your omelet?
Bob Hope:	I do, and I like having coffee in the morning with breakfast. It can be black, with no sugar in it.
Groucho Marx:	Can I get you anything else? I'll be right back.
Bob Hope:	I'll take my check also, please.
Groucho Marx:	I hope I didn't make it too hot. It is black though, and matches your tires.
	Let's have a big round of applause for Mr. Bob Hope, and I hope he pays the check.
	Our next contestant is Mr. John Lennon.
	John, are you willing to bet your life after death?
John Lennon:	I am, although I am not a betting man.
Groucho Marx:	I'll bet I can make a bet with you. All you have to do is say the secret word, and

	you will win the top prize of $1,000. Is it a deal?—or I can keep it for myself.
Announcer:	The secret word is [**JUICE**].
John Lennon:	It's a deal. What if I don't guess it? Do I have to pay you $1,000? All I have is $900 on me.
Groucho Marx:	I'll take the $900 and call it even. Here is the $900 question: *"What was your favorite breakfast?"*
John Lennon:	I didn't eat breakfast until afternoon.
Groucho Marx:	I may have won $900.
John Lennon:	All I had in the morning was a cup of coffee, and I had a few cigarettes with it.
Groucho Marx:	I had a cigar with mine, but that made it very soggy.
John Lennon:	I tried that, but it extinguished my cigarettes, and made it very hard to relight them.
Groucho Marx:	Is that all you had for breakfast, John?
John Lennon:	I had a lot going on in my head in the morning, making me not be hungry. I had a lot more coffee though.
Groucho Marx:	Nothing else in the morning, other than coffee and soggy cigarettes that would not light after dunking them?
John Lennon:	Not usually, no. Did I win $1,000?

Groucho Marx: No, but you did win a new silver cigarette case from A & M, our prize sponsor. Keep it always around your coffee, and you will never have soggy cigarettes again.

Let's have a big round of applause for Mr. John Lennon.

Now, Mr. George Harrison. Did you eat breakfast how John didn't? 'All You Can Eat' should include coffee with cigarettes in it.

How come I didn't get a cigar case like John's cigarette case? I could have it engraved—"All you can eat and smoke in one drink."

Announcer, please...

Announcer: Tonight's question is, *"What was your favorite breakfast?"*

The secret word is [**JUICE**].

Contestants cannot see the word, and if they say the secret word, they will win $1,000.

Groucho Marx: I could not have said it any clearer. How about it, George? What was your favorite breakfast?

George Harrison: I had a lot harder time in the morning than John did. I did not get much sleep

	at night, and had little appetite in the morning.
Groucho Marx:	I had a lot harder time than both of you. I had a large breakfast making me want to sleep all night, and all day.
George Harrison:	If I had breakfast, it had to be hard-boiled eggs, with toast and grape jam on it.
Groucho Marx:	How could you eat eggs if they were hard?
George Harrison:	I chewed them, or I could always swallow them whole.
Groucho Marx:	Did it hurt to have hard eggs in your throat with nothing to drink?
George Harrison:	Maybe that's why I didn't have breakfast very often.
Groucho Marx:	How come? You could have had coffee with cigarettes and eggs in it.
George Harrison:	I know, but it would have made my cigarettes get eggs on them.
Groucho Marx:	Thank you, George. Here is a cigarette case from our prize sponsor, A & M. Don't put any eggs in it, or they will get cigarettes on them.
	Mr. Leslie Nielsen, did you stay up all night and have nothing for breakfast also?

Leslie Nielsen:	I had a late-night breakfast in bed, and my napkin was longer than me.
Groucho Marx:	How come I didn't have breakfast in bed? I could have had lunch and dinner too, and also coffee with a cigar in it. How about something to drink? Coffee maybe?
Leslie Nielsen:	Coffee would be nice. Thank you.
Groucho Marx:	Maybe I could get you a glass of water, or something?
Leslie Nielsen:	No, thank you. It is in my coffee.
Groucho Marx:	I should have thought of that—water with a little coffee, and a cigar in a cup.
	Thank you, Mr. Nielsen. I could have it in bed, and have my napkin folded up, and have it become a high-top table.
	Our next contestant has many high-top folded tables, Mr. Gene Hackman. Welcome back to Round 2 of *You Bet Your Life After Death*.
Gene Hackman:	Did I not win in the first round? I answered the question correctly, and it was objective.
	Could I have a subjective question, please?

Groucho Marx: I could have it all subjective with a subject, and you as its subject that it is subjected to.

First subject. I can't remember the subject.

Announcer, please.

Announcer: Tonight's question is: *"What was your favorite breakfast?"*

The secret word is [**JUICE**].

Contestants cannot see the word, and if they say the word, they will win $1,000.

Groucho Marx: All the contestant has to do is say the secret word. How about it, Gene?

Did you have breakfast in the morning— or late at night like the others?

Gene Hackman: I had it in the morning, like most people.

Groucho Marx: Like most people? How do you know when most people have breakfast?

I could ask them all, but I'm afraid of what they'll say. I may have to have the breakfast menus changed to say, 'Evenings Only'.

Gene Hackman: I had a lot of coffee first, although I didn't have anything in it—just black. Then I'd have as my favorite breakfast,

	a bowl of fruit and a couple of hard-boiled eggs.
Groucho Marx:	How about more coffee, or anything else to drink?
Gene Hackman:	I could have some apricot nectar, or some hot chocolate if it was cold outside.
Groucho Marx:	Hot chocolate? How would that taste with a cigar in it? I'll have to try it.
	Thank you, Gene. I'll have my breakfast with hot chocolate, from now on—but I'm sorry, it did not include the secret word.
	You will have another chance in the next round of questions.
	Let's ask George Burns. *What was your favorite breakfast?*
George Burns:	I had a cigar, but in my mouth or in my hand—not in my coffee. How does it taste in the coffee?
Groucho Marx:	I'm having it in hot chocolate now. Would you like to try it?
George Burns:	No, I think I will have it in my mouth, or in my hand.
Groucho Marx:	Please tell the audience, George. What was your favorite breakfast?

	Say the secret word, and you will win $1,000—with a hot chocolate to go with the cigar in your mouth, or in your hand if you don't want it in the cup.
George Burns:	I had a lot of favorite breakfasts. It had to be hot though, for me to be hungry and eat it slowly.
	I liked a bowl of oatmeal with a lot of raisins in it.
Groucho Marx:	If it was hot, did you have something to drink that was not hot, to cool you off?
George Burns:	I did—a glass of apple or orange juice...
	[APPLAUSE]
Groucho Marx:	I didn't give too many hints, did I? You said the secret word, and won the $1,000 top prize from our prize sponsor,
	A & M cigarette cases—and also the fine Desoto-Plymouth dealers, all across America.
Announcer:	We have one winner of the $1,000 top prize for saying the secret word.
	The rest of the contestants are unable to hear or see the secret word, which is [**JUICE**].

Groucho Marx: Mr. Freddie Mercury... is that your real name, or did you have it custom-made? It could have been 'Groucho', you know.

Freddie Mercury: I had it custom-made, and 'Groucho' can be my middle name now—if I have your permission.

Groucho Marx: Have my permission? I stole it from a kid in kindergarten who called me 'Groucho'.

Freddie Mercury: I could be 'Grouchie', with an 'i-e' on the end of it, having all 'E' sounds at the ends of my names.

Groucho Marx: How come all 'E's'? Why not all 'O's, A's, I's, or U's'? You could have one for each day of the week.

Freddie Mercury: I could. All of them would be wonderful for me.

Groucho Marx: Can I call you 'Freddie', or is it with an 'O' today? Can I ask you an important question? *What was your favorite breakfast?*

Say the secret word, and you will win $1,000.

Freddie Mercury: I liked having a lot of apple juice in the morning...

[APPLAUSE]

Groucho Marx: And you said the secret word, "Juice." It ends in 'e', so it wasn't a fair question.

I am curious now. What else did you have for breakfast—an apple, or some scrapple? Any other words ending with an 'e'?

How about some cheese? I could make it an 'i' letter, you know. Macaroni, or how about some salami?

I like mine with a brownie, but that has an 'i' and an 'e' at the end.

Freddie Mercury: I like that, because my name is 'Freddie' with an 'i-e' at the end. I could make it another letter today, though.

Groucho Marx: How about if I give you $1,000 to go with your apple juice, both ending with an 'e'?

Freddie Mercury: I'll take it. Thank you very much.

Groucho Marx: Our next contestant is Mr. Bob Newhart. How are you, Bob?

Bob Newhart: I'm... I'm dead. Let me explain. I went to get something to eat, and... and I died.

It had its funny moment, because I didn't die until after I ate something. Not...not a lot of laughter, but it was funny to me.

Groucho Marx: I know what you mean. I had a meal like that once also.

Bob Newhart: If I had burped and died, it would have been funnier, but I didn't.

Groucho Marx: It didn't happen to be your breakfast, did it? I'm not saying it was your favorite breakfast, if you ate it and died—but tell us, what was your favorite breakfast that didn't kill you?

Bob Newhart: I... I have to hear the question again because I was distracted. I looked at the time, and my watch has been stolen.

Groucho Marx: How come you have a watch when there is no time here? It could be any time.

Bob Newhart: I had it on, and can't remember if my meal was breakfast, lunch, or dinner. It could have been a midnight snack.

Groucho Marx: I have a clue for you. Did you have anything to drink with your meal?

Bob Newhart: I did not. I died before I had a chance to drink anything, but there had been a glass of water near my plate.

Groucho Marx: I had a glass of water once. I had it without anything in it, other than my coffee. I have coffee in my water for breakfast.

	What had been your favorite breakfast, Bob? It can be anything, and if you say the secret word, you will win $1,000.
Bob Newhart:	I liked ham and eggs, although I am a vegetarian.
Groucho Marx:	How could you be a vegetarian if you liked ham and eggs?
Bob Newhart:	I decided it after I ate the ham and eggs, and died. I... I liked it though. Did I win $1,000?
Groucho Marx:	No, Bob. I will ask it another way. Did you have a favorite breakfast drink? I did, and it had a lot of water in it.
Bob Newhart:	I had a lot of coffee in the morning, on the days I didn't die.
Groucho Marx:	Thank you, Bob. I'd like to offer you something, but I don't have a watch on.
	Our next contestant is Mr. John Candy. Hello, Mr. Candy. Is that your favorite breakfast?—because that is my question.
John Candy:	No, I liked having all kinds of eggs with hash brown potatoes. What I liked most were eggs that had been fried in butter, or with some bacon.
Groucho Marx:	Did you have some coffee, or anything to drink with it?

John Candy:	I had a protein drink, with a lot of greens and a banana in it.
Groucho Marx:	Is there anything else? Hot chocolate, or some coffee with water in it?
John Candy:	I had a lot in the protein drink, so no, I didn't.
Announcer:	Our contest question is: *"What was your favorite breakfast?"*
	The secret word is [**JUICE**]. If a contestant says the secret word, they will win $1,000.
Groucho Marx:	Our next guest is Mr. George Carlin. His name begins with a 'G', and ends with a 'G'—just like mine, but his has an 'E' at the end, and mine has an 'O' with no 'G', just an 'H'.
	Hello, Mr. Carlin. Is there a favorite breakfast you would like to share? There are a lot of people here, I know—but they look pretty hungry.
George Carlin:	How could I feed them all? I would have a lot of dishes to clean.
Groucho Marx:	It could be a lot like an assembly line, except everyone would be in the line, and no one would be eating.
George Carlin:	I can have it all packaged and ready for everyone to take it home. I could also have it delivered.

Groucho Marx:	Drinks also? I'd like mine to be delivered.
George Carlin:	I could arrange all of that. I am God having a dream of creating all that I desire—like in life.
Groucho Marx:	I have a contest question, and if your answer has the secret word, you will win $1,000. Here is the question: *"What was your favorite breakfast?"*
Announcer:	The secret word is [**JUICE**].
George Carlin:	I liked almost any kind of eggs with toast, preferably darkened to be almost burnt.
Groucho Marx:	How come you don't just eat it burnt, or on fire? It could be used to cook eggs on it.
George Carlin:	I could, but I could get a visit from the Fire Department while I am eating.
Groucho Marx:	Hot dogs and hot toast. How about some hot pepper on it, and they won't have to come back for lunch or dinner?
George Carlin:	I could have it with hot coffee or hot chocolate.
Groucho Marx:	With a lit cigar in it would really make it worthwhile for them. How about

	another drink—maybe something cold, or a large bucket of water?
George Carlin:	I could have a cold drink, I think—how about you?
Groucho Marx:	No, thank you. I had a drink in my hotel room but it had to be extinguished.

Hold up your hands and clap for all of our contestants on *You Bet Your Life After Death*. They deserve it.

If you have a drink in your hands, you can refrain from clapping. It could be dangerous if it happens to spill.

If it is the lava in a cup of java that I make, it never cools off.

Round 3

"How could all I had done
heal so many people,
and not myself?"

Groucho Marx:	Let's all welcome back our guests for Round 3 of *You Bet Your Life After Death*.
	Say the secret word, and you will win $1,000.
	Our contestants cannot hear the secret word, backstage where they are hearing the program.
Announcer:	Tonight's secret word is [**INSTANTLY**].
Groucho Marx:	The question to each of our contestants is, *"How could all I had done heal so many people, and not myself?"*
	Let's have both Mr. George Burns and Mr. Freddie Mercury begin, as they won the last round by saying the secret word.
	I'll bet you both $1,000 that I can get you not to say the secret word.
	George, how could all you had done heal so many people, and not yourself?
George Burns:	I didn't heal myself? I died, didn't I?
Groucho Marx:	How come it didn't heal you? It healed me when I died. I didn't have to die though—I could have lived on in eternity on the Earth until everyone else was gone, and be the only one left. That would have healed me—if I didn't have jokes to tell.

I'd be laughing at myself. How could I laugh at myself if there was no one I could find humor with?

I could die and go to heaven, and tell jokes like I am now.

How about it, George? How could all you had done heal so many people, and not yourself?

George Burns: All I had done healed so many people? I helped them to heal in their minds by halting non-funny thoughts with a funny thought.

Groucho Marx: I had a lot of non-funny thoughts that I tried to heal with a funny thought. One of them was funny.

How about you, Mr. Mercury? Can I call you "Mr. Mercury"?

Freddie Mercury: I like it, but I like "Freddie" much better.

Can I call you "Groucho," or "Mr. Marx"?

Groucho Marx: I like to be called "Groucho" before "Marx," but either way is fine.

Freddie Mercury: I healed many people with my music, and my hearing them cheer was healing for me. I loved it, and love heals me.

Did I win again? Winning heals me because I love it also.

Groucho Marx: I love your answer, but how did it heal you? Was it slowly?

Freddie Mercury: I healed instantly every time...

[APPLAUSE]

I did it again? I love it.

Groucho Marx: I love it too, but I may need to borrow $1,000 from you. How can I repay you?

Freddie Mercury: I may have healed completely now. I can make it a gift.

Groucho Marx: I love gifts. I could gift it to someone else, and they could gift it to someone else—then we would all heal, and no one would have $1,000—unless it came back to you or me again, at which time I would hold onto it.

Our next guest is Mr. Bob Hope. Do you like gifts, Bob?

I have $1,000 if you say the secret word in your answer. "How could all you had done heal so many people, and not yourself?"

I will love your answer, no matter what it is.

Bob Hope: I love your question. I healed in bringing a little bit of humor and levity to a lot of people, all certainly heading to their deaths—many in the near

	future, and the others further into the future.
	I loved doing it, but I did not love myself as much as I should have—like the time I had to borrow $1,000 from Groucho Marx.
Groucho Marx:	I had to borrow it from Freddie Mercury, so it wasn't mine, Bob.
Bob Hope:	I am "Bob" now? How about "Mr. Hope," as in "I hope he's going to pay me back?"
Groucho Marx:	It healed me, Bob. I hope it heals you in having paid it back—even if it was a gift. I could really heal being gifted with it twice.
	Did it heal you instantly? Oops, I said the secret word, so it makes your answer disqualified. You already have my $1,000.
	Announcer, let's have another secret word, and keep it a secret please.
Announcer:	The new secret word is [**HUMOR**].
Groucho Marx:	Bob, "How could all you had done heal so many people, and not yourself?"
Bob Hope:	I healed myself in hearing their laughter. I loved hearing it, because it healed me in healing them.

Groucho Marx: Did you borrow money from them too, Bob?

Bob Hope: No, I healed in having all of my free performances cost less than the others.

I could have charged less, but they were not free to me.

Groucho Marx: I could have charged less if you didn't borrow my $1,000. If "free" means they cost less, how could they be free?

Bob Hope: I could have borrowed a little bit from each person, then paid them to laugh. I would have been making a lot of money then, if I was not funny.

Groucho Marx: I think it could have cost more if you were not funny. I could loan you another $1,000.

Bob Hope: Cost me more? I think I'll keep my performances free.

Groucho Marx: Let's have a big hand for Mr. Bob Hope, and hope he makes a lot of money in his free performances.

Our next guest is Mr. John Lennon. Am I pronouncing your name right? "John," is it?

John Lennon: I am John, and not a walrus, as once believed.

Groucho Marx:	Not a walrus? Neither am I. I had been a penguin once, but was informed by my mother that I wasn't.
	I have a question, and if you say the secret word, you will win $1,000.
	The secret word is not 'Walrus', or you would have won $1,000 already.
John Lennon:	I am ready for your question, now that I know the secret word is not 'Walrus'.
Announcer:	The secret word is [**HUMOR**].
Groucho Marx:	*"How could all you had done heal so many people, and not yourself?"*
	If you can imagine that the secret word is not 'Secret' or 'Walrus', you have many to choose from.
John Lennon:	I healed in having my music heal in the minds of others, you know. It healed me also.
	Not healing kept me living to play more music.
Groucho Marx:	Did you have a lot of laughter in playing with bandmates, or in having conversations in the media? I didn't.
John Lennon:	I did. We had a lot of fun sometimes, but I always had a lot on my mind with all that was going on.

Groucho Marx:	How could it have been any more fun? It must have had a lot of funny moments.
John Lennon:	I could have laughed at it all, because it made me think of its absurdity. I made it an absurdity by healing others, and not myself.
Groucho Marx:	I laughed at an absurdity once, but an absurdity has to be funny, so it didn't count.
	Thank you, John. I would applaud for you, but it would be an absurdity since I am the host.
	Our next guest is Mr. George Harrison. Hello, George. I had another contestant named 'George' here—actually, there are two more.
	Maybe I could have all 'George' contestants, and the secret word could be 'George'. It would be an absurdity, but it might also be funny. What do you think?
George Harrison:	I think it would be funnier if I won the $1,000.
Groucho Marx:	If you say the secret word, you will win the secret word—which has $1,000 attached to it.
Announcer:	The secret word is **[HUMOR]**.

Groucho Marx: Contestants cannot hear the secret word in the backstage room, where they are now.

George, how could you not hear the secret word if you are not in the backstage room with the others?

George Harrison: I did hear it, and I find it absurd being here where I can hear it.

Groucho Marx: Announcer... my announcer is 'George' also, making 4 of you. Let's have another secret word, and it can't be "George"—or maybe it can, and I won't tell them about it.

Announcer: The new secret word is **[POSSIBLE]**.

Groucho Marx: Okay, George. Are you George #1 or George # 2? I lost count.

George Harrison: I was "George" in my life, but now I am "George in the Mind of God," so I would be "George One."

Groucho Marx: "George One"? I could be "Groucho One"—at least I hope there's only one.

George Harrison: I am one in my life, and One with a capital "O" in the Mind of God—making me always "George One."

Groucho Marx: How could I be "Groucho One" in the Mind of God, if God is also "George One, Two, Three, and Four"?

George Harrison: It is all possible in...

[APPLAUSE]

Groucho Marx: George #4, George #1 said the secret word, which is "Possible"—and not only possible, he actually did it.

How about $1,000 for George Harrison? Is that possible?

Announcer, please—what is our new secret word?

Announcer: The new secret word is **[ALLOW]**.

Contestants cannot hear or see the secret word.

Groucho, our next guest is Mr. Leslie Nielsen.

Groucho Marx: Hello, Mr. Nielsen. Welcome back to our show. If you say the secret word, you will win $1,000—except I just gave it to George. He has to divide it 4 ways.

Leslie Nielsen: I can always allow you to borrow it from all of them.

[APPLAUSE]

Groucho Marx: I can't allow you to win that fast. I'll have to borrow money from 'the 4 George's', and everyone in the audience.

Leslie Nielsen: I will allow it. Did I win another $1,000?

Groucho Marx:	I hope not. I can't allow it, or afford it.
	Announcer, allow us to have another secret word, but one that is allowed—and not "Allow."
Announcer:	The new secret word is **[WILLING]**.
Groucho Marx:	Mr. Hackman, is it? Can I call you "Gene"?
Gene Hackman:	I can be called "Gene," if you would like to call me.
Groucho Marx:	I am calling, and I lose money every time I call someone, it seems.
	Gene, if you say the mostly secret word, you will win $1,000. Is it a deal, or am I making a big mistake?
Gene Hackman:	It's a deal. How can I find out what the secret word is?
Groucho Marx:	How can you find out what the secret word is?
	Ask anyone—they all know.
Gene Hackman:	I could always use my God-like insights, now that I'm dead—although I'm God-like, I'm not going to cheat.
Groucho Marx:	I am God-like also, but I'm going to cheat to get my money back.
Gene Hackman:	I could help you, and we'll be God-like cheaters with a lot of money.

Groucho Marx: I met people like that, and they were not God-like at all—not after I cheated them.

Okay Gene, have I made it clear now? "How could you heal so many people, and not yourself?"

Gene Hackman: I did heal myself. I died, didn't I?

Groucho Marx: I don't know. Am I talking to a dead person? I could be—I mean, that's what dead people keep telling me.

How did you heal others, and not yourself—before you died?

Gene Hackman: All I could do was be an authentic person, even though my life was about playing many other characters, including villains.

I always had a grounding mechanism within myself as a reference point, and it allowed me to be myself when I wasn't acting.

Acting was just that—acting.

Groucho Marx: I acted once, and was told not to act up like that. I have acted down, ever since.

Thank you, Gene.

Our next contestant is Mr. Bob Newhart.

"Bob," is it? Can I call you "Bob" for short?

Bob Newhart: I am called "Bob" for short, and "Mr. Bob" for long.

Groucho Marx: Hello, "Mr. Bob for long," as long as we're not being short.

I have a new secret word, and it is not "new" or "word," but it is a secret—but everyone knows it except for you and the next contestants.

If you say the secret word, and I have borrowed enough money, you will have won $1,000.

What do you have to say, "Mr. Bob for long"? I could have made it a lot shorter, but I didn't want to let him have a chance to speak. He might say the secret word.

Bob Newhart: I... I could hear someone in the audience thinking the secret word. Am I disqualified?

Groucho Marx: Actually, I will ask you another question so you don't go away empty-handed.

"How many deaths does it take for one person to heal?"

Bob Newhart: I'd... I'd like to hear that again please. I wasn't paying attention. I... I got distracted hearing the secret word.

It had a lot of other words with it. I can't repeat most of them though.

Groucho Marx: I know where you heard them, and I didn't mean to think those things.

I will call you "Bob for not so long" now, or just "Bob for short."

"How many deaths does it take for one person to heal?"—and ignore all of those other words you are hearing.

Bob Newhart: I... I don't know. I only died once, so don't know for sure. Maybe I could die again and see what happens.

Groucho Marx: Die again? Do you mean we can all die again? I don't want to die again, but I guess if I want to live again, I'll have to die again—after getting my money back using my God-like powers.

Bob Newhart: I would like to live again, but not in my dead body. I would have to be propped up so it wouldn't look like I was already dead.

Groucho Marx: I could hold you up as a coat rack, but not for long—I would need to get my coat and go out once in a while.

Now for our next contestant, Mr. John Candy.

Where does the name "Candy" come from? If I had to pick a name, it would be "Candy," but just for the first name—

	unless my last name was "Cane," or even "Candy" like yours.
John Candy:	"How could I have healed so many others, and not myself?"
Groucho Marx:	I'll ask all the questions. If you have a question, please raise your hand. I will call on you when it's your turn.
	Okay, did you ask a question—or did I ask a question and you questioned me with another question that was the same question?
John Candy:	I asked, *"How could I have healed so many people, and not myself?"*
Groucho Marx:	Are you asking me? I don't have any answers—I'm just trying to get my money back by asking questions, but can see now that it's not going to work. How about if I answer my own question, and you give me money?
John Candy:	How about if I ask your question, and you ask my question—and we both keep answering with the same question?
Groucho Marx:	How about if you give me money, and I give you money—until one of us stops asking the same question—which is also the answer?
John Candy:	I'll be the first one to ask with an answer, and answer with a question.

Healing myself was the hard part; healing others was easy.

Healing myself meant I had to always feel love for myself, and then I could give it all to others.

That is how I could have healed myself when I healed so many others.

Groucho Marx: How could I come up with a better answer as my question being an answer? I can answer that with a question.

How could I heal myself if I don't have an answer? I can heal myself by not having a question—and then I don't care if I have an answer—and I could never have won $1,000, and would have to borrow it.

I think I know the answer now—have no question and no answer, and it will be enough—there's no question.

Our next guest is George #4, I think. I lost count after George #3. I counted all of them, but forgot one and had to start over. It was one in the middle, but it couldn't have been because one isn't in the middle—not even close.

How about it, Georgie? I can call you "Georgie," and I won't get confused again—or maybe I should call you "Georgie 1," in case more will be coming. I have no idea at this point.

"How could you have healed so many people, and not yourself?"

George Carlin: Did I heal anyone, or heal myself? I don't think so.

They healed on their own, and just had me as an excuse. Why me? I have no idea.

I could have reminded them how I couldn't heal what they needed to heal, and it was humorous for them to hear it from me.

I think that's it—I didn't heal, and they thought it was funny—and they healed in their realization of it being funny.

I may have had a healing moment or two from their healing from it, but I wasn't having any part of being healed in life.

I would have run out of material in my mind to find humor with. I needed an edge. Having a need to be healed was my edge.

Groucho Marx: I had an edge once, and it wasn't very sharp. Actually, it was a very dull edge—and all I could hope for was to have a not very sharp, dull angle instead. That is my dullness angle without any sharp edges.

I can't cut to the heart of the matter with it, though I certainly try.

Let's have a dull round of applause for all of our guests on *You Bet Your Life After Death,* brought to you by all of the Desoto-Plymouth dealers, all across America.

Round 4

"What do I miss most in life,
that I cannot manifest in heaven?"

Groucho Marx: All of our guests have been invited back—including me—for whatever reason, to another round of hostile questioning by me... now I remember—I am the hostile questioner named "Groucho."

Announcer: Groucho, in Round 4, each contestant will be asked one question, and have a chance to win $1,000 if they say the secret word. All of our contestants cannot hear or see the secret word, now on your screen.

Tonight's secret word is **[HEALING]**.

Groucho Marx: Here comes our first contestant, a two-time winner already—Mr. Freddie Mercury. I can borrow some money, can't I?

Freddie Mercury: I can loan it if I know what the secret word is.

Groucho Marx: I can loan you all the words in my vocabulary, then you will have all the secret words.

If I give you all the secret words, it may have to be a $2,000 loan.

Freddie Mercury: I will have a lot of words. I will have to think about it.

Groucho Marx: I have one question, with a lot of words—while you are thinking about it.

	Announcer, what is our question? I have too many words to remember.
Announcer:	The question is: *"What do I miss most in life, that I cannot manifest in heaven?"*
Groucho Marx:	How about it? It's a lot of words, I know.
Freddie Mercury:	I do not miss my life, in heaven. I loved it, but I do not have any wish to be in it again.
Groucho Marx:	I would—if I had a lot of secret words, and $2,000.
Freddie Mercury:	I know, but I like it here in heaven.
Groucho Marx:	I do too, but how could I have anything to buy with my $2,000?

I can't buy anything here—mainly because I don't have the money I plan to borrow from you.

Thank you, Freddie. I'm sorry I didn't give you more words that contained the secret word, but hang onto them.

You will have more chances to win, and I'll only use words in my vocabulary.

Our next guest also won in the last round. That's how we do it here—bring them right back because they have all the money I gave them. Maybe I can get it back by not giving away all the secret words.

George Harrison is back, or is it 'Georgie 2'? I don't know—I lost count after Georgie 1.

George Harrison: Hello, I think I am 'George 1'. I can't remember either.

Groucho Marx: You didn't forget that I gave you $1,000, did you?

George Harrison: I'd never forget that—I mean, unless I couldn't remember.

Groucho Marx: I'll borrow it, and forget. Then we'll be even and forget the whole thing.

George Harrison: I'll keep it, and forget to loan it. Then I will be even, and forget the whole thing.

Groucho Marx: Okay, it's a deal—but I forgot what we agreed on.

George #1 or George #2: *"What do you miss most in life, that you cannot manifest in heaven?"*

Say the secret word, and you will win another $1,000.

George Harrison: I miss my life of having nothing I needed, except a little healing and peace of mind.

[APPLAUSE]

Groucho Marx:	Congratulations. You did it again. You said the secret word, which is "Healing".
	You have another $1,000 to forget about.
	All across America, you will find our sponsor—the fine Desoto-Plymouth dealers.
Announcer:	Groucho, our next contestant is also a winner in the last round—Mr. Leslie Nielsen.
Groucho Marx:	Hello, Mr. Nielsen—or should I call you 'Leslie', or 'Mr. Leslie Nielsen', or just 'Mister'?
Leslie Nielsen:	Call me 'Leslie', but not 'Mr. Leslie'. It could get confused with all the other 'Mr. Leslies'.
Groucho Marx:	Are there other 'Mr. Leslies'? I didn't know that—but now I know, and will likely be confused.
	Leslie, I will ask you one question, and if you say the secret word, you will win $1,000.
Announcer:	The secret word is **[HEALING]**.
Groucho Marx:	Here's the question: *"What do I miss most in my life, that I cannot manifest in heaven?"*

Leslie Nielsen: I am on a game show. I missed the 'Heaven' exit.

Groucho Marx: I missed it too. How did I get here anyway?

I'm sorry, Leslie—you have more chances to win.

Speaking of exits, all across America, you will find our sponsor—the fine Desoto-Plymouth dealers.

Announcer: Groucho, our next guest is Mr. Bob Hope. He has not won in any of the earlier rounds.

Groucho Marx: Hello, Mr. Hope. Or is it 'Bob'?

Bob Hope: I hope it is. I have a lot riding on my being in heaven.

Everyone thinks I'm dead, and must be in heaven.

Groucho Marx: Me too. Well, not in heaven, but another 'H' word.

Bob, how about I ask you a question, and if you say the secret word, I'll give you $1,000.

Is it a deal? Heaven is full of good deals.

Bob Hope: I am ready for your question.

Groucho Marx: I am ready for your answer. Announcer, what is the question again?

	He has a job to do. That was our deal.
Announcer:	The question is, *"What do I miss about my life, that I cannot manifest in heaven?"*
Groucho Marx:	Take your time, even if there is no time here.
	Alright, have you come up with an answer? Talk amongst yourself.
Bob Hope:	I miss that I had a lot of friends, and a lot who were not. It made me a better judge of character.
	Here, I can instantly know a spirit's character as its individual aspect of God, as you could also.
Groucho Marx:	I could, but I am an aspect of God that has no needs—except for the money I have been giving away.
	Thank you, Bob. We could have been friends, if you didn't know about my character.
	Announcer, let's bring out another character—or one of Bob's friends.
Announcer:	Groucho, here is Mr. George Burns. He has not won anything yet either. Let's welcome Mr. Burns.
Groucho Marx:	I'll bet he is one of Bob Hope's friends. Hello, George 2 or 3. How can I help

you, other than give you our secret word—which only one contestant has said so far. It was George 1 or 2, to be exact.

I will ask you one question, and if you say the secret word, you will win $1,000—and it can be any word, as long as it's the secret word.

Announcer: The secret word is **[HEALING]**.

Groucho Marx: George 2 or 3, *"What do you miss most about your life, that you cannot manifest in heaven?"*

George Burns: I missed my Gracie, but we are in heaven now, so I cannot miss her, like in my life.

Groucho Marx: I'd miss her too, if I knew her—but I didn't. I missed out on a lot, I know—but I don't miss it.

I miss the money I gave away though. Thank you, George 2 or 3. How about if we just go with 'George 2-1/2'?

George 2-1/2 and Gracie makes one. That is how my math adds up.

I look forward to seeing you on *You Bet Your Life After Death* in another round, where I don't win my money back.

I can win it back, and I won't miss it.

Announcer:	Groucho, our next guest is Mr. Bob Newhart, and he hasn't won anything in the earlier rounds of questions.
Groucho Marx:	I can help him win, and then get my money back.
	How many Bobs do we have? I am on #2 now. I can't count higher than that before getting confused.
	Hello, Bob 1—I mean, 2. I lost count.
Bob Newhart:	I... I can help you. I am Bob 1, but I came back after being Bob 2 in the last round, and Bob 1 in the first round, and Bob 2 after that.
Groucho Marx:	I can't remember more than two, so how about if we just keep it as 'Bob', just having one name, in two rounds, with another name in any other rounds—as long as it is not 'Bob'.
Bob Newhart:	I... I could be 'Bob' in all of the new rounds, and another 'Bob' in all the old rounds—and tell you I changed my name... and see if you notice any difference.
	I... I had done that before, and it worked. No one noticed that I changed my name.
Groucho Marx:	I can't remember now if I asked you the question, or gave you the secret word.

I'm not going to give it to you now, because you may try to change it, and then become 'Bob 1' again, and pretend that you didn't hear it.

Announcer, please give us the secret word that cannot be changed, and don't let Bob 1 or Bob 2 hear it.

Announcer: Groucho, our secret word is **[HEALING]**.

Groucho Marx: It had been a secret... what is the not-so-secret question?

Announcer: Groucho, tonight's question is, *"What do I miss most in life, that I cannot manifest in heaven?"*

Groucho Marx: I have $1,000 if Bob One or Bob Two says the secret word. I can wait. Decide which 'Bob' it will be.

Now I can't wait—how about it, both Bobs?

Bob Newhart: All... all I miss from life had... had to be holding onto it for so long. I mean, I can't hold onto life here at all.

It is an illusion that has healing as its objective, and as its outcome.

[APPLAUSE]

Groucho Marx: You said the secret word, Bob 1 and 2. How are you going to split the winnings?

	I'll help you—let's make my name 'Bob' also, and we'll split it 3 ways. I'd go higher, but the numbers get confusing.
Announcer:	Groucho, our next contestant is Mr. John Candy.
Groucho Marx:	Hello, Mr. John, is it? Did you decide on it in the last minute, like Bob did?
John Candy:	I did, but it hadn't changed because it was John before—for my whole life, I mean, including in my life after death.
	Despite what it appears, I am in my life after death.
Groucho Marx:	I am too, and somehow got this job of being a quiz show host. I don't know how I got it—I guess my name made it less confusing who is the host—being called, 'Groucho', as opposed to 'Groucho 2 or 3'.
	All I can do is ask the questions, and if you say the secret word, I will give you $1,000—and we can still be friends.
	Could I make it any more appealing—other than not being friends?
John Candy:	I guess I could be friends, even if I don't win $1,000. I mean, I could be—I didn't say "I would be."

Groucho Marx: I guess I could be too, but I'll have to ask Groucho #2. He annoys all of my friends, because they're not my friends anymore.

I will ask Groucho #1 to ask you to answer this: *"What do I miss in my life, that I cannot manifest in heaven?"*

Think about it—and I am not in your answer, because I'm not one of your friends.

John Candy: *"What do I miss in my life, that I cannot manifest in heaven?"*

Groucho Marx: I can ask it again—unless you want to. I will ask Groucho #1 to ask it in a less annoying way.

If I can have your answer, I will be listening in an annoying way.

John Candy: I am always asking myself that same question. I mean, "always" in eternity, if you know what I mean—and I never have an answer.

I can manifest anything here that is healing...

[APPLAUSE]

Groucho Marx: I can answer it for you. Now you have $1,000, and no answer.

I'd like to win $1,000, and not have an answer. Then I could afford to have

	more questions and no answers for eternity.
	I may never have an answer in that arrangement. Congratulations, I hope I can borrow your $1,000, and leave you with only questions.
	I could look for the answers in my spare time.
Announcer:	Groucho, our next guest is Mr. Gene Hackman. He has not won in the earlier rounds.
Groucho Marx:	Let's ask him "Why not?" in an annoying way.
	Maybe he'll say the secret word, and I won't have to ask him any more questions.
Gene Hackman:	I can answer that one—because I didn't say "the secret word," but now I did—so, I must have won $1,000 for saying it.
	I must have had it coming to win this time.
Groucho Marx:	I must have had it coming too... or going—it came and went. How can I get it back? I will ask Gene.
	Can I call you 'Gene', or 'Mr. Hackman', or 'Mr. Gene Hackman' for short?

Gene Hackman: I am called 'Gene' mostly—in my life, and in my life after death.

Groucho Marx: I am called 'Groucho' in my life, and in my life after death. I can't get rid of it. I should have picked a better name.

How about if I ask you a question, and if you say the secret word—which is still a secret—I will give you $1,000.

At least our sponsor will—your Desoto-Plymouth dealers, in every state of the union.

Gene Hackman: Can I have the money first, or does it have to be after I say the secret word?

Groucho Marx: I don't have an answer for you. I'll ask it another way, in the first person. *"What do I miss in life, that I cannot manifest in heaven?"*

Think it over. I'll give you a few seconds, not an eternity.

Gene Hackman: All I miss is having my things around me in my home—which I collected in my lifetime. They each had a special meaning for me, and is why I collected them. I miss having them, but I kept each one's meaning in my heart and soul.

Groucho Marx: If you kept each one's meaning in your heart and soul, how could you miss them?

Gene Hackman: I found them healing in life, which gave them meaning.

[APPLAUSE]

Groucho Marx: Gene, you did it. Now you can begin a new collection of meaningful memories. I may have to call the game early.

Everyone is winning now. I don't know how many winners I can afford.

Announcer: Groucho, our next guest has not won in any of the earlier rounds—Mr. George Carlin.

Groucho Marx: I'll call him 'George #4', or is it #3? I get confused after #2.

George Carlin: I am all the numbers you want to give me. I can handle all of them, ad infinitum.

Groucho Marx: "Ad infinitum?" What does "ad infinitum" mean? I could use it as a secret word sometime—except it sounds like 2 words, and 2 is my limit with numbers—and with words not in my vocabulary, which has about 10 words already. I will ask it another time, being at my number and word limit now.

George—that I can't remember which number—I will ask you a question, and if you say the secret word, it will be the end of my quiz show because I will be out of money. Is it a deal? —Or I can continue on without giving you any prize money, even if you say the secret word—one word, mind you.

George Carlin: It's a deal—if I can keep the money, and loan it back with interest, ad infinitum.

Groucho Marx: "Ad infinitum?" There it is again. How can I agree to something with words not in my vocabulary?

I can agree not to agree—that's still an agreement.

Alright George, I agree not to agree—and I will ask all the other Georges not to agree either, and I will agree to it.

Here is my question, but it is really your question. I am giving it to you—but not the answer. I don't have an answer.

It is only something you can answer, George—and if you say the secret word, you will win $1,000.

"What do I miss in my life that I cannot manifest in heaven?" Go ahead, think it over. I can wait.

George Carlin: I miss that I can't make people laugh in heaven. They all know what I'm thinking, so it isn't funny to them.

Groucho Marx: People know what I'm thinking, and it IS funny to them that I'm not thinking. Let's both think about it, and it will not be as funny, but it will be half funny.

Thank you, George # 3-1/2, now that I'm doing half of the thinking.

Announcer: Groucho, our next guest is Mr. John Lennon. He has not won in any of the earlier rounds.

Groucho Marx: Hello, John. I mean John #2, having been John #1 in the last round.

John Lennon: Hello, Groucho. I am here for a second chance—or maybe it's my fourth chance. I lost count after you got me doing math in my head.

Groucho Marx: I can't count, but I can remember. I remember that I lost count. It was after #1 or #2, I can't remember.

John Lennon: I can remember how to count, but what can I count now except God's loving, healing instances that I had in my life?

[APPLAUSE]

Groucho Marx: John, you did it, and you ended my career as a quiz show host. How can I repay you?

	I needed a career change that doesn't require counting.
John Lennon:	How about if I host the show for you?
Groucho Marx:	I can arrange that, if you give me $1,000. I didn't even ask you what you miss in life, that you cannot manifest in heaven.
John Lennon:	I miss that I could create music in life, and people could listen—and it would heal their minds if it made them feel better.
Groucho Marx:	Can it heal them if you make music here in heaven, and they don't hear it?
John Lennon:	It can, but it has to be music that they hear in their souls, or even in their dreams.
Groucho Marx:	How can I hear it in my dreams? I don't remember my dreams.
	I must have them, even if I don't remember. It's not that I don't remember, it's just that I forgot.
	Congratulations, John #2, is it? I forgot which number to use, and if I used it already.
Announcer:	Groucho, all of our contestants will be returning for Round 5 of *You Bet Your Life after Death*.

Groucho Marx: Five? That's a big number, like the 5 winners we had in Round 4, and 3 winners in Round 3.

At least those numbers are all the same, except for number 4—which is not a number I had learned yet, since it is after 3... but I did learn 5. Maybe that is why I got confused.

All across America, you will find a friendly Desoto-Plymouth dealer—in every state of the union.

Round 5

"How can I heal myself in my afterlife?"

Announcer:	Groucho, in our next round, contestants will be asked one question, and can win $1,000 if their answer includes the secret word. Tonight, our secret word is **[MANIFEST]**. All of our contestants have won in the earlier rounds, except for Mr. George Carlin and Mr. Bob Hope. They will be the first contestants.
Groucho Marx:	All across America, you will find our sponsor, and in every state of the union—visit your local, friendly Desoto-Plymouth dealer. Hello, Mr. Hope. How can I help you? I can give you a question, and hope you will win $1,000 if your answer contains the secret word. If you say the secret word, I will lose $1,000. I cannot win in this deal—I can only hope not to lose.
Bob Hope:	I can hope I win, and hope you do not lose- making me always 'Mr. Hope.'
Groucho Marx:	I can hope, and hope, and hope—making me 'Hope #3', I think. I may have lost count. I get confused after #2. Bob, or maybe I can call you 'Hope #2'. Then I may not get confused.

Hope #2, where was I? I will begin again. If I get confused you can stop me, and I will begin again, again.

Here is tonight's question, and it is not confusing—only to me, unless I forget—then it is less confusing because I forgot, and it doesn't matter.

Beginning again, here is tonight's question: *"How can I heal myself in my afterlife?"*

I know, it's not confusing, but it can be if your answer is not one containing the secret word.

I will leave it at that, and see if it does, or not. It will contain a lot of other words, and that is what is confusing.

Bob Hope: I hope it contains it. That's not it, is it?

Groucho Marx: George Fenneman, is the secret word 'It'?

Bob Hope: I don't mean 'It'. I mean 'Contains'. Is it the secret word? How could it not be if my answer contains the secret word?

Groucho Marx: I was confused before, but now I hope I lose, so I can forget. I will begin again, again.

Hope #1, and Hope #2: *"How can I heal myself in my afterlife?"*

	I can always begin again, again, again, Mr. Hope 1 and 2.
Bob Hope:	I can heal myself in my afterlife by imagining that I am a bird, and everything I look at heals me—if I love being the bird spotting it.
Groucho Marx:	I am healing in my afterlife by not being a bird—I had been a penguin once, until I was told that I wasn't.
	It healed me, although my mother didn't mean it to be healing.
Bob Hope:	I am healing in my afterlife as a bird, although I can be anything that I choose to be. I could be a penguin, and heal as God keeping me cool.
Groucho Marx:	I could have healed as a cool penguin, but my mother hadn't thought of that. Her son, the penguin, wasn't cool at all.
	Let's ask Mr. George Carlin. George, can I call you 'George' now? I lost count and have to begin again in my 'George' counting—until I get confused and have to begin again, again. If I don't get confused after number 2, I may just forget.
George Carlin:	I can help you in your counting, and in your forgetting. Don't count, and don't

keep anything in your mind that is not worth remembering.

I always had a lot to remember, but it was worth remembering. Now I am an integral part of God having nothing but love, so it is impossible to forget.

It is all that there is, and all that I am. How could I forget if it is "all that there is"?

Groucho Marx: I don't know if I can remember "all that there is" because it sounds like a lot.

I did learn that it is only one though.

George Carlin: It is one, because how could it not be only one?

It cannot be less than one, or more than one, if it is "all that there is."

Groucho Marx: Good, I can count it then—and hope it is not "ad infinitum" or anything, because it is not in my vocabulary, even if it is "all that there is."

George, I have one question, and only one: *"How can I heal myself in my afterlife?"*

Announcer: Groucho, tonight's secret word is **[MANIFEST]**.

Groucho Marx: How about it George 1, and only 1?

George Carlin: I can heal myself in my afterlife by allowing only one thing into my mind—LOVE... and it's the only thing I can allow into my mind, because it is "all that there is" in the Mind of God, where I am healing myself as an aspect of God that had dreamed I wasn't.

Groucho Marx: I had a dream once that I wasn't, but I couldn't remember—that's how I know I wasn't, because if I was, I would remember.

Announcer: Groucho, our next guest is Mr. Freddie Mercury, and tonight's question is, *"How can I heal myself in my afterlife?"*

Groucho Marx: I will tell you how I heal myself, if you want to know. I ask guests one question, and I heal when their answers are not confusing—or have a lot of words that are not in my vocabulary.

If they do, I forget, and heal anyway—so either way, I heal. How can I not heal? —I also know the secret word.

I could heal more if I won $1,000 though, and had nothing left to heal.

Let's ask Freddie—he looks like he needs to heal.

Groucho Marx: Hello, Freddie. I can't remember if you allowed me to call you Freddie #1, or is there another number?

Freddie Mercury: 'Freddie #1' would be perfect for me.

Groucho Marx: Freddie #1, I will ask you one question, and if you say the secret word, I will give you another $1,000, and have to find another occupation. I will heal, although I would heal a lot more if I had the $1,000.

Freddie Mercury: I can heal a lot more having the $1,000, so I think I may have to win.

Groucho Marx: Have to win? You mean, I have to lose. What do you mean, you "have to win"?

Freddie Mercury: I will heal if I win, and you will heal if you lose—so I have to win for both of us to heal.

Groucho Marx: Now I am confused, and I will have to lose to heal... "heal my money back" is what I need to heal.

Freddie Mercury: Exactly.

Groucho Marx: Freddie #1, answer this question, and if you say the secret word, you win another $1,000—and I lose and heal—maybe even heal it back, but our quiz show isn't set up that way.

Here is tonight's question: *"How can I heal myself in my afterlife?"*—without having Groucho lose anything.

Freddie Mercury: I heal myself by allowing God to heal me, which also heals Groucho, because we are all one.

Groucho Marx: Good. Now I hope you win, because I can't lose—I'll just have $1,000 less.

Freddie Mercury: I must not have won this time, but healed just the same.

Groucho Marx: I must have healed, because I'll keep the prize money.

Thank you, Freddie #1.

Announcer: Groucho, our next guest is Mr. Bob Newhart.

Groucho Marx: Hello, Bob. How can I help you? I am giving away money, but you will have to say the secret word, and it will no longer be a secret—unless it's not made public for a few days, and we'll keep the audience in suspense.

I can agree, if you answer the question, and I am not confused by it.

The question is, *"How can I heal myself in my afterlife?"*

Bob Newhart: I... I can heal... I just don't know the answer.

Groucho Marx: You don't know the answer? I don't know it either.

All you have to say is the secret word. How come you don't know the answer?

Bob Newhart: I... I had an answer, but I healed in my afterlife, so I don't have that answer anymore.

Groucho Marx: How did it heal you when you had the answer?

Bob Newhart: I healed because I had the answer, so I didn't need the question... that means it wasn't an answer at all.

Hear... hear me out on this. How could I have an answer with no question?

I had to have a question, but now you are asking me, and... and I'm healed, so I do not have an answer.

I had it, but it healed and went away.

Groucho Marx: I healed and went away once, but I ended up here.

I had $1,000, but it healed and went away once too—and not just once. I lost count after the second time.

Bob Newhart: I healed when I ate something and died, but it's not the same kind of healing as eating something and not dying...

	I... I mean not dying is healing, as well as dying... but not with food in your mouth.
Groucho Marx:	I had food in my mouth, and $1,000 in my pocket. What a delight. Now I am in eternity, losing $1,000 over and over again.
	Is it healing me? I hope so, I keep getting more money from our sponsor, your Desoto-Plymouth dealer, in every state, all across America.
Announcer:	Groucho, our next guest is Mr. Gene Hackman.
Groucho Marx:	Hello, Mr. Gene Hackman. Can I call you that? I called someone else that, and they ignored me.
Gene Hackman:	I am called that all the time, but I am not in time anymore. I am in timelessness, and lovingness.
Groucho Marx:	I am not in time anymore either, so cannot have a good time. I can have a good timelessness though.
Gene Hackman:	I can have a goodness in time, and in timelessness.
Groucho Marx:	I can have it too, if I could have some time. I can only have timelessness now, because I had my good time.

	I can have it as, "Goodness gracious, how did I get from time to timelessness?"
	I'll tell you about it, but I don't have any time right now.
Announcer:	Groucho, our guests all have a chance to win $1,000 if they answer one question, and say the secret word.
Groucho Marx:	I can also give them enough time to answer it. Alright, Mr. Hackman—time's up.
	Here is tonight's question: *"How can I heal myself in my afterlife?"*
Announcer:	Groucho, the secret word is **[MANIFEST]**.
Gene Hackman:	I manifest healing...
	[APPLAUSE]
Gene Hackman:	I manifested healing?
Groucho Marx:	You manifested $1,000 away from me, but it is really from the Desoto-Plymouth dealers, all across America.
Announcer:	Groucho, our next guest is Mr. George Burns.
Groucho Marx:	Hello, Mr. Burns, and welcome back. How have you been? Did you bring the money back, or did you spend it timelessly? I'll bet you he spent it and is coming back for more.

	How about it, George? Or is it 'Mr. Burns'? I can't always remember.
George Burns:	Hello, I am back for more—and you can call me 'Burns' or 'George', as long as I'm within hearing distance.
Groucho Marx:	Hearing distance? How can I know if I am within calling distance? You didn't hear the secret word, did you?
	I can't have it heard, and if it is heard, I can't have it remembered.
George Burns:	I didn't hear it, but I can hear it if you call it to me. I am within "calling it, and forgetting it" distance.
Groucho Marx:	I have heard that, but I didn't want to repeat it. I will call you one question: *"How can I heal myself in my afterlife?"*
	I called it, but don't forget it—not for a little while. There is no time here, so a little while is forever.
	How about it? Give it to me straight.
George Burns:	I heal myself by always allowing myself to have God in my thoughts, because I am an aspect of God, and God is all there is.
	How could I not heal by having God in all of my thoughts? I do not know, because it is not even possible.

	How could something be impossible to God? It is an illusion that only I can heal by thinking about God.
Groucho Marx:	I'm sorry, I thought it would include the secret word, and I would give you $1,000, but it isn't possible.
	What is possible is that I keep it, and then I can have more possibilities—if I had some time.
Announcer:	Our next guest is Mr. John Candy.
Groucho Marx:	Hello, Mr. Candy. Can I help it if I like your name? I love candy.
	It goes with my cigar, but only in my coffee for breakfast.
	I can also have my coffee without candy, but it is a lot better without the cigar sticking out.
	I will ask you one question, and if you say the secret word, you will win $1,000 and I will have no candy money left—so I may ask you for some, if you happen to say the secret word, and win.
	Is it a deal, or do I have to get my candy now, before it's too late?
John Candy:	I think I'll get some now too, before it's too late.

	I mean, I could get some now, and then get a lot more later, after I win.
Groucho Marx:	I like that idea—and then I can get some from you, after you win.
	It could be a win-win situation, but only if you win. All you have to do is answer one question, and if you say the secret word, I will be a lucky winner.
	Can I ask you the question now, or is there something else I can win if you say the secret word? —Or I'll just take the money instead of the candy.
	Here is the question: *"How can I heal myself in my afterlife?"* I can ask it another way, but it only has one way.
John Candy:	I heal myself in my afterlife by not having anything I need or want—and I heal not because I need or want it.
	It is because all I can be here in my afterlife is healed... not that I'm in an afterlife, because life is a dream.
	How could I be in it? I imagined it—and imagining it had its healing moments, as you can imagine.
	I imagine that I can be anything, and I am. How could I not be anything if all I am is all that there is?

Groucho Marx: I was a penguin once, but my mother said I wasn't. Now I'm confused.

John Candy: I can help in that regard. I can be a penguin too, but only if it heals me. I found a lot of healing in comedy, so I did a lot of comedy—allowing me to heal in hearing people laughing.

It was a lot of hard work, but it was healing—so healing can be hard work sometimes.

Groucho Marx: I did hard work once, but it wasn't healing. I had a penguin costume on, and I couldn't hear very well what my mother was telling me to do.

John Candy: I can see how that wasn't very healing.

Groucho Marx: I could have healed if I heard what she was saying, but I was in a tub of ice.

I only heard her saying, "OH MY GOD!"

John Candy: I heard that, being an aspect of God and all.

Groucho Marx: I can give you something to heal, but you don't need it—so I won't. I can give you some advice though—if you can imagine anything, you can become anything. So, imagine all that God has inserted into your imagined dream is all there to heal you—and then you will not need anything.

	The beauty of that is, what heals goes away, and is not inserted into your dream anymore.
Announcer:	Groucho, our next guest is Mr. Bob Hope again. He said that he imagined he is coming back to win.
Groucho Marx:	I thought he doesn't need anything if he is healed—or maybe he didn't heal because he didn't know the answer. Let's ask him. How come you want to win, Bob?
Bob Hope:	I imagined that I won in this round, and I didn't—so I didn't heal by manifesting...
	[APPLAUSE]
Groucho Marx:	Are you healed now, Bob? I lost a lot of money on your imagining and healing.
	How can I manifest it in an instant like you did?
Bob Hope:	I imagined it, and I am God—so it manifested.
Groucho Marx:	How come I'm not a penguin anymore? My mother would have had a hard time unmanifesting that one.
Bob Hope:	I healed and won, so now I don't need anything. Can I leave now? I mean, I need the money first.

Groucho Marx: I thought you didn't need anything. How could you need it if you don't need it?

Bob Hope: I imagined having it and not needing it, which is how I manifested my having it.

Does it make any sense—to imagine having it, which makes needing it unnecessary?

It is always the same—in time, or in timelessness.

Groucho Marx: I imagined having a tub of ice, and I didn't need it—but I never imagined my mother pulling me up by my arms so fast—not that I could have prevented it... or maybe I could have. If there had been some soap and hot water, I would have been okay.

Announcer: Groucho, our next guest is Mr. George Harrison.

Groucho Marx: Hello, George. Our announcer is 'George', so I will call you 'Harrison'—or I will call him 'Fenneman'. Which do you prefer? I could call you both 'Harrison and Fenneman', and leave all 'George' names out of it. How about it, Harrison?

George Harrison: How about if I call you 'Marx' instead of 'Groucho'? Then no one gets

	confused, because 'Groucho' is a common name, you know.
Groucho Marx:	I know—I've heard it a lot, especially when I was within hearing distance.
Announcer:	Tonight's secret word is **[MANIFEST]**.
Groucho Marx:	Alright, Harrison, tonight's secret word is still a secret, but only to you and the next contestants.

Let's bring out our next contestant, since Harrison is an accomplice of John Lennon.

I will ask you both a question, and you both have one chance to answer.

If your answer includes the secret word, or one that sounds exactly like it, our prize sponsor will give you $1,000 since I don't have any money left over. I could also give you some candy instead.

Here is the question: *"How can I heal myself in my afterlife?"*

Only one answer for you both, and half of the prize money for each, if you win. Talk it over.

Harrison and Lennon are coming to terms on the prize money, I think. Have you decided on how much candy each of you will get?

George Harrison: I have an answer, and you might not like it. I manifest in my afterlife a lot differently than John manifests in his.

[APPLAUSE]

Announcer: Groucho, we have a pair of winners for saying the secret word.

Groucho Marx: How much candy does that set us back, George? I mean, Fenneman.

I can manifest more candy—but I need it, so maybe I can't. I'll sweeten the pot. Tell the audience how you both manifest differently, and I'll throw in the candy.

George Harrison: I can manifest in my afterlife by imagining all that I needed to heal in my life—which is some peace and privacy, and what I manifest is healing myself. John manifests in his afterlife by forgiving himself for all that he thinks he could have done with more love for himself and others.

Announcer: Groucho, our next guest is Mr. Leslie Nielsen.

Groucho Marx: Hello, Mr. Nielsen. Am I saying that correctly? Or is it NY-elson, with a silent 'i-e' making a 'y' sound?

Leslie Nielsen: Leslie has an 'i-e', making a 'y' sound.

Groucho Marx: I didn't hear that, because it's a silent 'i-e', but I'll take your word for it.

Leslie, which is silent after the second 'l', but it makes a 'y' sound—I will ask you a question, and if you say the secret word, you will win a piece of candy—and $1,000 if I can come up with it.

Is it a deal, or do I need to get the money first?

Leslie Nielsen: I cannot agree to it until I hear the question.

Groucho Marx: Here is the question, with no silent letters—in case you are wondering if it is a trick question.

"How can I heal myself in my afterlife?" I know it is a lot of un-silent letters, but give it your best shot.

Leslie Nielsen: I can answer it in one word, with one silent letter—'Love' with a silent 'e' at the end, unlike the silent 'i-e'.

Groucho Marx: How could a silent 'e' be unlike a silent 'i-e' that sounds like a 'y'?

I have a silent 'i-e' in my name, but it is also invisible, and it sounds like an 'o'—but you don't hear it, and it's next to the other 'o' which has a sound, and sounds like an 'o'.

Leslie Nielsen: I don't know—which has a silent 'k', and a silent 'w', which are visible.

Groucho Marx: How are we supposed to know they are silent, if they are visible?

I was silent and visible once, but I didn't like it.

Leslie Nielsen: I know—with a silent 'k' and a silent 'w'. God is all there is, which is not silent, and it is visible.

"All there is" is also silent and invisible. How could it be both silent and un-silent; visible and invisible?

It is all coming from your mind—where the invisible becomes visible, and the silent becomes un-silent.

It is up to each of us for it to be God, or not.

Groucho Marx: Thank you, Mr. Nielsen—with an 'i-e' that sounds like an 'e'. That is not only confusing, it is visible, which makes it more confusing. It wouldn't be so bad if it was silent and invisible—but it's after the first 'n', and the one after the second 'n' is silent and invisible.

Announcer: That concludes our program—brought to you by our sponsor, your local Desoto-Plymouth dealer, from coast-to-coast, in every state of the union.

Join us on the next episode of *You Bet Your Life After Death*.

Afterword

Groucho Marx: All I can add in my life-after-death quiz show is that I had lost a lot of money by asking a lot of questions. I will keep my asking a secret from now on.

John Lennon: I allow him to ask secret questions, if I can have the secret word.

George Harrison: I have a lot I can add, but it's a secret.

Bob Hope: I hope it's not always a secret, because I need to win some more money.

Leslie Nielsen: I had heard that, but I cannot keep a secret.

Gene Hackman: I had heard it too, so it's not a secret.

George Burns: How can I make it a secret again?

Freddie Mercury: I can keep it a secret, if it is no longer allowed to be known.

Bob Newhart: I... I wouldn't have known if the secret had been well kept.

John Candy: I could always have it become my closing statement, but I want it to be a secret also.

George Carlin: I could have it as a secret that is healed, and it will disappear like all of my other healed secrets. That is how it is, and how it will always be.

About the Author

From God Mind:

*Paul Gorman illuminates as a spiritual researcher,
writing his discoveries into books,
allowing healing in the minds
of all who read them.*

Groucho Marx: I am all about having authors, but how could I be the host, and him be the author?

John Lennon: I authored a lot in here—John and Paul, you know.

George Harrison: I authored a little bit myself, and now I'm on the Author Page.

Bob Hope: I hope I can be one of the authors, or my laughs would be for nothing.

Leslie Nielsen: Am I an author? I did not know that until I was asked about having to sign this book.

Gene Hackman: I am an author, but have only collaborated on this one book in my afterlife.

George Burns: I am an author having healed my mind, so I have nothing to write. I can always think of something though.

Freddie Mercury: I am an author, and I am loving it!

Bob Newhart: I am a healed author in my afterlife, but hear... hear me out on this—I can't heal if Gorman asks me for more to write... because I'm dead.

John Candy: I am dead in my afterlife also, but I can give my words to Gorman for him to make a book—I mean, if it's a good book.

George Carlin: All authors have one, and only one thing in common—they have your interests at heart, because having their own interests at heart would only make sense if they made a lot of money. This book may make a lot of money, but only because it has your interests at heart.

www.ingramcontent.com/pod-product-compliance
Lightning Source LLC
Chambersburg PA
CBHW030557080526
44585CB00012B/402